WINDOWS

First published 2007 by
Worple Press
PO Box 328
Tonbridge
Kent TN9 1WR

Copyright © Individual contributors

The right of the contributors to this anthology to be identified as the author of this work has been asserted by them in accordance with the Copyrights, Designs and Patents Act, 1988. All rights reserved.

British Library Cataloguing in Publication data.
A catalogue record for this book is available from the British Library

ISBN 978 1 905208 14 2

Worple Press is an independent publisher specialising in poetry, art and alternative titles. **Worple Press** can be contacted at:

Worple Press
PO Box 328
Tonbridge
Kent TN9 1WR

Tel: 01732 368958
E-mail: theworpleco@aol.com
Website: www.worplepress.co.uk

Typset and printed by Q3 Digital/Litho, Loughborough, Leicestershire

WINDOWS

AN ANTHOLOGY OF POEMS
FROM THE TONBRIDGE
POETRY COMPETITION 2007

CONTENTS

JUDGES' FOREWORD AND REPORT

YOUNG PRIZE-WINNERS AND POEMS
First Prize

Jack Lindsay *The Window of my Mind*	15

Second Prize

Megan Snyders *Eliza Lane*	16

Third Prize

Harriett Hughes *Cold*	18

Commendations

Emily Robotham *Windows*	19
Aileen Freer *The Window*	20
Chloë Jeremy *Window*	21
Hannah Cross *The Strange Man*	22
Molly Richard *Separate*	24
William Raven *Looking through a window at myself*	25
Holly Tobin *Windowmaker*	26
Luke Fraser *Window*	27
Jonathan Highgate *Looking through windows*	28
Edward Smith *Sunday Summer Delights*	29

ADULT PRIZE-WINNERS AND POEMS

First Prize
Caroline Price   *Last Call*   33
Second Prize
Jenny Morris   *Going Back*   34
Third Prize
Anna Davis   *Broomfaulds Crescent*   35

Commendations
Phil Powley   *I, too, remember Adlestrop*   36
David Grubb   *Three Priests on Their Way*   37
John Arnold   *Freshers Week*   38
Michael McCarthy   *Learning*   39
Mike Casey   *Blurred Divide*   40
Patrick Moran   *Leavings*   42
Terence Brick   *Suibhne returns to Cnoc na Dail*   44
Gavin Stewart   *Insomnia*   46
John Foggin   *Is Sixteen*   47
Paul Webb   *The Apprentice*   49
Ann Drysdale   *Thirteen Syllables of Safety*   50
Ian McEwen   *Badly Trained*   51
Josie Turner   *Civil*   52
Will Kemp   *E.K.*   53
Julian Stannard   *Bringing Mussolini back to England*   54
Kate Rhodes   *Al Musayyib*   55
Jeremy Duffield   *Close*   56
Geraldine Mills   *Reading my Father's Hand*   57
Madeline Munro   *Lapwings*   58
William Wood   *Do you want to hold him?*   59

Notes on Contributors   60
Notes on Judges   64

JUDGES' FOREWORD

It was a pleasure to judge this competition. Or rather, competition*s*: and quite different experiences, maybe because the younger group were constrained by a theme. The best of these 'window' poems are excellent, as you'll see; surprising, moving, imaginative, really alive – though it has to be said with the others we often found we were comparing like-with-like. So that the contrast when we came to the variety of the 'open' section was striking – which brought home that in some ways it's quite arbitrary, judging one poem against another, and we know that others would have chosen differently. Certainly there were a *lot* of good poems, and actually we enjoyed reading every entry. Nevertheless we're confident that these are our favourite poems – and we hope you'll agree that they are outstanding.

Open Section

All three main prize winners happen to tell a story or have a narrative running behind them, though just as important to us was the freshness and texture of their language and ideas. These are well-made poems that spoke to us straightaway and that we got more out of every time we read them.

First prize: 'Last Call'. This is surely a winner in any company. It is moving, direct and not at all sentimental; and though completely unshowy, it's quietly virtuoso too, not least in how it develops and releases its imagery; and ambitious actually, but never likely to be pretentious, (literally) grounded as it is – all that 'rhubarb thickening' and 'stray sprouts and onions/run to seed'. We love all that rich real detail. And the fact that, right from the start, it's a poem that draws the reader in, makes us part of its world:

Look past the house where strangers live
and across the lawn: in front of the poplar hedge,
that's where she buried his ashes …

That's good isn't it, 'where strangers live', so that we know in three words this is someone's former home; and by the third line we understand the relationship and what has happened. The poem continues

                      … in the ghost
of a vegetable garden, no more now
than a rectangle of deeper green –

From here the garden becomes an extended metaphor; but let's stay with just this first stanza. That bold enjambment 'ghost/of' for instance keys us into the quite weighty ends of lines: 'strangers live', 'poplar hedge', 'no more now' and 'deeper green' – each of which carries some figurative meaning. Even the 'poplar hedge' has a subliminal effect, because it's a boundary (in a poem about the ultimate boundary) and also because it makes us think of people – poplar being from the Latin, apparently, *populus*. And then what about the 'deeper green' – deeper because buried, the garden no longer something organic, living and making live ('vegetable' from *vegetare*, animating), but instead reduced to the two dimensions of a shape.

'Last Call' goes on to recount how over time the garden became encroached upon as the man worked it less each year – 'thistles soon pushed up, and red dead-nettle, speedwell;/gradually a showing of all the wild flowers from around.' Then there is the final 'outburst' of popies that caught his wife's eye – 'a dancing line of red', a surprised and surprisingly positive image – and one that accords with the feeling all the way throgh what is very much a life-affirming poem.

We hope this (rather rushed – so much more we wanted to say) discussion suggests not just why 'Last Call' came first, but also gives some idea of how we were thinking as we worked through the entries. Now to turn necessarily more briefly to the other prize-winners. 'Going Back' stood out for us at once. It is so well-made, and so direct and yet atmospheric too; such an evocative poem, and one that like 'Last Call' celebrates where it might have regretted or mourned (you'll notice it too coincidentally ends with bitter-sweet dancing). And, like a dance, 'Going Back' is both highly patterned and spontaneous – a sonnet so deftly handled that it manages to speak naturally and fully, restraining and (therefore) heightening the emotion.

We loved 'Broomfaulds Crescent' too. The confidence to title it after a (presumably) real place persuades the reader this is a real experience; the concision and lyric eloquence of the piece are tremendous; and the wonderful images - 'Flour fell like snow from my hands' for instance and that surprising fox trapped at the end … It's an extraordinary poem.

There are so many things we wanted to say about the commended poems – so many things we noticed and talked through – but it will have to be enough here to note that, different though they are from each other, every one of poems in the list made an impact, and that a handful might easily on another day have been in the top three.

Younger Poets

Again the outright winner seemed to us genuinely remarkable. Despite its title, 'The Window of My Mind' is surprising – and surefooted – at every turn; the language is always interesting, the images unpredictable but satisfying. One unusual feature in this poem is that it begins by looking *at* windows; 'round ship's windows' seen from a distance like lanterns, before giving us a series of windows looked *from* – green country windows, and half-open windows giving on to 'long shadows of evening, and the moon rising in a dusky blue sky'. These first three, rather beautiful instances come up against the contrast at the emotional centre of the piece, hospital windows from which 'I look out on concrete and a rubbish-strewn railway line. I am never well but I have the strength to long for home.' The poem stays in this place then, as it must – 'I look out like a prisoner at a dry land' (which made us think again about the ship's windows) – until the narrator finds solace in memory and imagination, when s/he closes her eyes to 'look from the morning windows of home' – where, defying the dry land, 'dew sparkles in lush grass'. All of these images are deliberately stylised, heightened from life, but they manage still to be personal, not received or hand-me-down.

There's a maturity and confidence here that is impressive but which isn't trying to impress; not least in the shape of the poem, a set of prose lines that counterpoint the pattern of each 'I have seen' and 'I look out' statement. 'The Window of My Mind' would have held its own in the 'open' category.

The second and third place poems, 'Eliza Lane', and 'Cold' are formal in another and more traditional way, since both are ballads. Not surprising then that both tell stories, too; 'Eliza Lane' giving us a completely unexpected twist at the end – such a strong poem because of the flexibility of the language within the form, and the specific contemporary detail; and it promises even better in the probably very near future.

'Cold' is older in style and language (the poet has evidently learnt from 'Reading Gaol'), but like 'Eliza Lane' makes very striking – and appropriate – use of the form; we found it a haunting piece, and moving – the ending especially, the perfect repetition in ' … there are those that love and love/Even when the window's closed'.

Finally, about the commended poems – all of these (and several other entries actually) made a real impression on us, and two or three of which (though a little uneven in themselves) were clearly the work of very gifted writers. We hope and trust the excellent Tonbridge Competition will continue to inspire and encourage the wealth of writing talent in Kent and Sussex, and we thank all involved for allowing us to read and respond to the work this year.

Ann and Peter Sansom

YOUNG PRIZE-WINNERS AND POEMS

THE WINDOW OF MY MIND

I have seen the round ship's windows, like individual lanterns, burning softly as the boat glides over dark waters.

I have gazed out of green country windows, at sunlit May fields and the cow parsley bloom.

I have watched through half-open windows the long shadows of evening, and the moon rising in a dusky blue sky.

Now from hospital windows, I look out on concrete and a rubbish-strewn railway line. I am never well but have the strength to long for home.

From this window I look out like a prisoner at a dry land. Bars stripe my skies these days.

I close my eyes and once again am looking from the morning windows of home. Wild flowers are opening and dew sparkles in lush grass.

I journey to that haven, framed by ivy-covered glass: the window of my mind.

Jack Lindsay
Aged 13
Robertsbridge Community College

ELIZA LANE

A young girl dressed in yellow,
With ribbons in her hair,
Looked out upon the outside world
And thought of being there.

She turned back to her sister,
Who lay across the bed;
The sister silently sat up.
"What do you see?" she said.

The yellow girl smiled sweetly,
And looked through the glass pane.
She started to describe the views
Down Eliza Lane:

"I see the Blackbirds flying,
And nesting in the trees.
I see the flowers set in rows
With buzzing bumble bees,"

"The sky is splashed with colour;
The clouds are pearly white,
Some children playing in the field,
Flying a purple kite."

The girl in yellow bade goodbye.
Her sister rose from bed;
She threw the window open wide
And leaned against the ledge,

The sister gazed through the glass,
Down at Eliza Lane,
Where plastic bags flew in the breeze;
Everything drenched in rain,

The air, heavy with thick smog,
Refused to let in light;
The car park housed a gang of youths
Who set a bin alight,

The sister smiled and thought of
The young girl's words before,
Since the truth could not compare to
What the blind sister saw.

Megan Snyders
Aged 14 years
Tunbridge Wells Girls' Grammar School

COLD

I never really understood
The place, what it could do.
The silent men who walked in white
Through rows ; just pew on pew.
Where when the lonely need escape
From a world that can not care,
They go and tread sweet paradise
Even when there's nothing there.
I stayed a while there in the dark
Didn't feel the hours pass,
Until the sun began to set
Bathed red through coloured glass.
I turned my head to look out through
Beyond the window pane,
I saw a figure rising up
From a plot that filled with rain.
Twas just a woman standing still
Dressed head to toe in black.
She'd lost her son, her only one
She'd never bring him back.
To sit and watch her for a while
To memorise her face,
You see she lives with countless more
Their grief, their fear, her space.
So who are we to stop and sit
And feel life left us old?
When there are those that love and love
Even when the window's cold.

Harriett Hughes
Aged 16
King's School, Canterbury

WINDOWS

A long way away
From warm summer nights,
Stands Old Grey Cottage.
Though the wind howls round
And damp has taken
Hold, for the woman
Sitting abandoned
In the old Bay, the
View is worth the cold.
Biting cold. Through her
Cataract-veiled eyes,
Windows of her soul,
She sees fantastic
Things. The sun always
Shines in her mind's eye.

She dreams of horses,
Running through the snow.
She sometimes sees kings
With jewelled turbans, who
Talk with trees. Pirates,
Who burn, scorch, live, die.
She dreams of cities
That rise and fall to
Dust. Penguins that slip
And slide on distant
Hills. Gold, diamonds, gems,
Ships, flags, battles, death..
And she knows someday,
As she looks through her
Weeping windows,
Her boy will come back
From France.

Emily Rowbotham
Aged 15 years
Sevenoaks School

THE WINDOW

There's a window on our classroom,
It's different.
Others don't notice,
But I do.

It sparkles whilst it's raining,
It gleams in the sun.
Others don't notice,
But I do.

There's nothing special about it,
This doorway leading to another world.
Others don't notice,
But I do.

Someone broke the window,
They had to change it.
Others didn't notice,
But I did.

This new window is dull,
It doesn't shine or gleam
Others don't notice,
But I do.

Aileen Freer
Aged 14 years
Robertsbridge Community College

WINDOW

What is the capital of Spain? Chloe……..*Chloe*

History, Science, Geography
It doesn't really matter to me,
They all have a window, they all have a view
So gaze and that's all you have to do.

I see the rabbits skip and dash
At the sight of danger, gone in a flash.
Down in the meadows, there sways a tree
It seems like simple peace to me.

I slowly drift off, but no matter how much I stare,
There's nothing I can do to get me there.
Then a sudden jolt, I'm back in my chair
And then I'm facing my teacher's stern glare.

Chloë Jeremy
Aged 10 years
Vine Hall School

THE STRANGE MAN

At night my heart leaps out of its cage,
For I see a ghostly figure in my window.
Tucked up in my cosy, warm bed
I try to count sheep,
But that figure stays there the whole night.

Sometimes I see a whole army of unearthly creatures
Screaming a silent scream,
Marching a still march.
Why can't they just leave me alone?
I'm only a child of eleven.

Why haunt me for I'm a quiet girl?
In the day nothing appears in my window
Just the odd bird and fly
For my window looks out onto a busy street
And no one can get in and out of my window.

I don't feel safe when in my room
In fact I try to hold off going to bed.
I close my clear window and shut my tinted curtains
So I can't see out of my weird window into the dimly lighted street.
But every night at around half past nine

My curtains fly open and I see the ragged old man
Standing there all night.
No matter if it's raining; he still is there
I try to creep into my mum's bed
But she says I'm too old for telling stories.

I do believe he lived here,
The figure in my window.
But now at night I go to my window and open it
For I am eager to try and contact him.
But each night he stares blankly into my room not even blinking.

I hope he leaves me soon for I do not get a wink of sleep when he is there,
Staring through my window.

By Hannah Cross
Aged 12
Ashford School

SEPARATE

Her hands shake as I watch her waiting.
She's prepared as she enters.
It never gets easier.
He takes his seat, tears fall down her face,
His hand reaches to touch her.
The window between them prevents emotion.
It doesn't allow reality.
And they talk. Stifled words come to the surface
Quickly swallowed again.
The glass glistens.
The light catching it allows an odd beauty to pass over
The couple it separates.
It doesn't fit.
The sentence was two years.
A window; the simplest penalty against love.

Molly Richard
Aged 16 years
Lavant House School

LOOKING THROUGH A WINDOW AT MYSELF

I went to bed last night
And as I slept I dreamt
That I was looking through a window
And I could see a plane go by
Flying very high up in the sky.

Someone was looking at me
Through the window of the plane
And it was me, but older.

I was on the plane
And I looked out of the window
Down to the ground, a long way down
A saw a little boy looking through a window
Up at me…

William Raven
12 years old
Dover College

WINDOW MAKER

He took the sand off summer's beach,
He took the ice from winter's beard.
And without a sound,
He jumped the cloud,
That hangs between the seasons.

He whipped them up; like angel's tears,
In a pot of solid sunlight.
And in the blaze,
Of Lokï's gaze,
A perfect frit was formed.

He blew it dry with winds whispers,
And shaped it with his voice.
And the glass was made.
But was his window complete?

No.
Not yet.

With a view on each side;
One calm and one wild,
A sunset or storm,
A sea or a lawn,
It would have purpose.

But the Window Maker sighed,
As he finally realised,
That, what is a window without its wall?

Holly Tobin
Aged 14 years
Tunbridge Wells Girls' Grammar School

WINDOW

Looking through the dusty and dirty glass into the gloomy, bleak office,
Smoothly rubbing my squeegee across the thick glass,
Sadly watching the silent drama going on inside,
I clean the windows of 24 Floyd Street.

Carefully adjusting my weight on the worryingly unstable ladder,
Quickly glancing at the long drop,
Slowly looking back at the dull men in dark suits,
I clean the windows of 24 Floyd Street.

Suddenly noticing a ghostlike image of myself looking at me,
Sneakily trying to stop him copying my every move,
Jerkily wiping the sweat dribbling down my cheek,
I clean the windows of 24 Floyd Street.

Quickly grabbing on to the window ledge,
Rapidly looking round at the train thundering past,
Happily laughing at my stupidity, my ghost laughed at me too,
I clean the windows of 24 Floyd Street.

Unhappily watching the mugs of coffee shake,
Gloomily glancing at a man typing on a PC,
Uninterestingly staring at a guy at a water dispenser,
I don't like cleaning the windows of 24 Floyd Street.

Luke Fraser
Aged 12 years
The Judd School

LOOKING THROUGH WINDOWS

Some look through windows and see
White sand and turquoise seas.
Others view rolling downs;
With the Long Man of Wilmington upon the hill.

Some look through windows and see
Great sand dunes rolling like waves on the sea.
Others observe great snow-topped mountains
Or heather clothing the ground.

Some look through windows and see
Scorching plains dotted with prickly cacti.
Others look on great tall office blocks
Or golden fields of hay.

And this is what some see,
On the route of the golden bumble bee.

Jack Highgate
Aged 13 years
Robertsbridge Community College

SUNDAY SUMMER DELIGHTS

My window looks out onto a world of Sunday summer delights,
Dad sleeps on a sun lounger,
while my sister creeps up with a bucket of freezing water.
My mother working hard as a donkey,
weeds the flowerbeds which she finds therapeutic.
In the corner of our plot of land I spy father's masterpiece –
the compost heap, the nourishing rot and mould of the garden,
full of furry bananas and death defying smells,
it lies there steaming with the heat,
that my father worked so hard at, to make his hot heap work.

In the undergrowth green eyes meet mine,
an evil stare that cuts me up.
They stare me down and move forward
and our cat minces out of the bushes.

Edward Smith
Aged 15 years
Sutton Valence School

ADULT PRIZE-WINNERS

LAST CALL

Look past the house where strangers live
and across the lawn: in front of the poplar hedge,
that's where she buried his ashes, in the ghost
of a vegetable garden, no more now
than a rectangle of deeper green –

he had begun, even before he died,
to let his plot grass over, its edges draw in,
the rhubarb thickening, stray sprouts and onions
run to seed, the furrows littered with potatoes
tiny as knucklebones; each year

turning some earth but working it less,
allowing rough grasses to sow themselves
and pigeons and pheasants pick their way
undisturbed, depositing other seeds
so that thistles soon pushed up, and red dead-nettle, speedwell;

gradually a showing of all the wild flowers from around,
though nothing as prolific as the poppies she saw
that next morning, that were suddenly there
catching her eye from the kitchen window,
an outburst, a dancing line of red.

GOING BACK

This seaside ballroom's where the dance-band played
below glass chandeliers and arching palms
where hearts could trip as hopes could be betrayed
and lust might turn to love in strangers' arms.

Now plaster cherubs on the ceiling smile
with broken lips to see the scene below.
A passing lame old girl can't reconcile
this empty night with those of long ago.

She hears faint melodies, remembers when
this was the most exciting place in town.
She whirled in gauze along the ranks of men.
But now all's derelict and falling down.

In this sad place of lost desire and chance
in darkness, by herself, she starts to dance.

BROOMFAULDS CRESCENT

My nose pressed against the glass,
stars were faint in the cold,
roses out front, uniformly drying.

Nothing moved, there were no cars
in the quiet cul de sac
that led up from the wood.

I wore a green striped apron,
wrapped in a warm smell of baking.
Leave the window, child.

Flour fell like snow from my hands.
I was looking along the road,
past orange-lit walls

and houses circling the green,
to where a fox crouched in his cage,
on the corner, beside the garage.

I, TOO, REMEMBER ADLESTROP

He sat across from me, slumped in a corner seat.
A soldier from the Front, care-worn, half asleep,
a book of poems on his knee. His uncapped brow
glistened in late June's heat.

Then, unexpectedly, the through train stopped
at a country halt. He stared outside. I coughed.
He closed his eyes and smiled, and all the cares
and fears of war slid from his face as birdsong
filled the carriages.

And so he stayed until the train pulled out,
the summer's sounds drowned by the engine's roar.

I turned, and through my window saw fields
of ripe corn sweep past, and poppies, beckoning.

THREE PRIESTS ON THEIR WAY

This one is bouncy and shaped like a bell;
his hair has been stolen by the birds to make their nests;
he is going to a civic dinner and has to make a speech
which means he will have to cut back on the wine;
he would like to tell them about the state of the roads
and why the hospital must never be closed but then
for years he has wanted to tell his one good joke;
he speeds up, he must not be late; will there be dancing?

This one has chosen to walk through the woods,
to embrace the view of daffodils, to approach the town
from the top so that he can see the steeples and towers
and flags and the flashes of sun on the river;
he has been asked to say The Grace and wonders
if Latin would be suitable, or something lighter about
fishes and dishes, or should he simply say Thank God?
He does not like the Mayor and his zipper grin.

This one wishes that he had not been invited;
perhaps there will be a sudden death and he will
be called away or one of the Chain Gang will fall
ill and he will be called to sit in the ambulance;
perhaps there will be a power failure and what
if one of the others were to fail to turn up; would
this mean that at last he could make his speech
about clowns, about the make up, about the tricks?

FRESHERS WEEK

Driving home, wiping drizzle,
the back seat still folded down:

*she seemed happy
as we left*

('goodbye' pecks
deliberately brief)

*Flatmates nice enough…
anything we forgot?*

PC, TV
up and running;

pens, pads, posters,
her favourite soft toy;

freezer, fridge, cupboard crammed
with food, old crockery and pans…..

A stack of emptied crates and holdalls
fidgets in the load space.

M25, Junction 10:
the traffic slows. We sigh.

Through the windscreen
brake lights turn to tears.

LEARNING

You remember nothing about grammar, or maths except seven times tables: *seacht fe seacht sin dahad a naoi,* and nothing at all about Irish apart from that. Or English, or poetry, except for Padraig Pearce: *Mother Ireland I have loved thee with a love that knew no fear.*

Bits of history: 1014, Brian Boru beating the Danes at the battle of Clontarf. Domnal O Sullivan's march to O Rourke of Breiffne after breaking the siege. *The Annals of the Four Masters* had the sound of a book you'd like.

Religion: Catechism class. The Master talking about immodest dress, you wondering what class of a dress was that? Parables, 'put them into your own words' – there was a farmer one time had two sons.

Compositions: but not what they were about or what you wrote. Ink wells, ha-penny nibs, Teresa Dennigan licking the ink off hers for fear she'd make a blot. Her mouth all blue like she was after eating blackberries, and her big brother Peadar pouring a full inkwell down his throat like men throwing back a glass of whiskey at a wake.

What you remember best: the slopes of the school yard and the high hedge, and the wall dividing the boys from the girls, and the hole near the gable, and eating your lunch, the bottle of milk and the taste of brown bread and blackberry jam, and the Regans having theirs out of a box, and O Brien's mother bringing him a boiled egg in a stocking to keep it hot.

Brigadier O Donovan arriving with a pile of *National Geographic,* and saying 'jolly good' this and 'jolly good' that, and the Master getting the class to stand up and sing *The Boys of Kilmichael,* a song the Brigadier said he'd never heard.

The bikes and riders in the *Ras Tailteann* whizzing past. One rider clinging onto someone else's handlebars. Another rider miles after everyone else. 'A puncture', Mickey Dineen said, 'either that or his chain came off. He'll never again catch up.'

BLURRED DIVIDE

Limber and loose-limbed, the orang-utan came,
pivoting on knuckles, from the back of the cage
to meet me at the plexiglass screen.
There were only a few centimetres between us
and less than two percent of DNA.

He showed his long incisors and hyena gums
and I displayed my yellow canine stumps.
Neither of us was overly impressed
or frightened by this show of virile pride.
Miserable wisps of orange hair sprouted
from his leathery, oak-tanned hide.
Miserable strands of grey streeled
across my crumpled parchment head.

He had a habit of drawing a cupped paw
all the way from cranium to chin,
dejected by everything around him,
all the empty chatter of visitors;
sometimes he would just hold his head,
as if he had a migraine coming on,
and use the paws as blinkers to screen out
all the pointless activity round about.

No wild man he, but more the old sad man
of the jungle where I had soldiered too;
we were a pair of codgers who needed time
to come to terms with past travails,
misdeeds—of which a multitude.
He sat, legs buckled; I crouched in mime,
Tried to accept the offered orange peel;
we were still eye to eye through the glass.
I saw cameos of myself inverted in the brown
pupils which hinted at defeated strength,
and fading recall of better times;
He may once have played and wrestled
with clinging young as I had done.

All different now, said the wise old face,
ineffably sad, lugubrious in its deepest folds,
knowing the game was up, of that no doubt.
He was; he stayed; this cage would see him out.

LEAVINGS
In memory of my father

You who loved to declaim
poems you'd learned at school
shied away from writing.

Just that note you left me
one day you went to town
for seeds and cabbage plants.

The words seeming childlike
in your unpractised hand:
Don't let the fire go out.

*

As a boy, I'd watch you
raking the fire; spreading
ashes over embers

so you could rouse at dawn
the quilted seed. I, too,
smouldered beneath your mould…

And yet, unfailingly,
I'd fill the bags of turf
to feed the archaic

solid fuel cooker.
And wait to sense again
all that was between us:

Dawn cold. The smoored ashes
shaken out. The makings
of a fire still intact.

*

Lilacs, leafing hedges.
The weeds raising bold heads.
Now, your spirit tempts me

to take up rake and spade,
the shears and watering can;
and use your remedies

for mildew and greenfly…
Yet I grumble, dither;
as if I were not meant

to step into your shoes.
But still you shuffle on;
kneel down and set to work.

Leaving behind plucked weeds;
your sowing clearer now
in the stirred, yielding clay.

SUIBHNE RETURNS TO CNOC NA DÁIL

(Cnoc na Dáil is Gaelic for 'The Hill of Debates')

Grey island. Green sea.
From port to starboard herring gulls drift,
salt salmon leap.

My face is stung by wind and spray
and in the trawling wake
are liquid seals.

Over Arran evening shadows fall
where honey buzzards
welcome me to furze and hazel.

I am king of all the animals,
of deer and stag,
badger, otter, stoat.

I praise the hare on the mountain,
I praise the hare in the gully,
it's good to praise the blue hare.

The torrent's voice commands
the king of blackthorn, mushroom,
wet pebbles, watercress.

Rowan berries fill my hand
in a gorge of brown water.
Leaf mould. Dark ravine.

Time was, men cowered before my gaze.
Now into the undergrowth
the stag strolls with ease.

I have been a beetle under bark
breathing decay.
I have been a ripening elderberry.

But I have been point of a sword,
barb of an arrow, shaft of a spear.
I have been solstice, equinox.

Now, with the deep set eyes
of a peninsular man I place my foot
in the Dunadd Stone and I am king.

INSOMNIA

The bloke on the door
        at the edge of the night
doles out our days,
              just one at a time

("each with its eyes, a hoist for the sun
and the requisite price for getting back in").

But I try to be fly,
take hold of his token,

                              with the sweat from my palms
I work it as clay.

        I mould it, control it,
my pains are my pension. My hands
full of futures, the blue prints for Rome.

I turn it and fire it
take a pleasure in glazing,

my day is a jar

                for the preserving of time.

And it holds, for a while; I am rich beyond reason;
though my bounty becomes tainted with the must of my sweat.

The doorman's a stickler; refuses re-entry.
He thinks with his body and smashes my pot.

IS SIXTEEN

'Is sixteen. Is bound as a putter, but unable yet to put. A year ago the horse ran away; knocked him off; trailed with the wagons. Off 10 months. Is lame now, and will always be lame. His leg was set wrong at first. One leg is shorter than the other. The pit makes him sick. The fumes make his head work.'

Evidence of a Monkwearmouth collier to the Children's Employment Commission 1842.

From Seghill, Silver Lonnen, Ledston Luck,
From Hartley's single shaft and broken crank,
They brought the stories of the colliers to book,

those grave and watchchained, whiskered men.
Listening, frowning, to the foreign tongue
of nervous pitmen, capless, ushered in;

like this one. Kay-legged. Broken by the pit;
sick with the sulphur rising in the shaft,
reeling, blind and dry mouthed. Cannot spit

the firedamp cobwebs closing up his mouth.
Wound up within the limits of the light
to shuffle in, and wet his lips, and tell the truth.

He cannot think. His head works so
in this rare air they seem to breathe.
His head works. Neither he, nor they would know

he speaks the tongue that Malory's Arthur spoke.
When Lucan wished to bring the king to town,
to leave the field to Mordred slain, his army broke,

and to the carrion men, the pillers, creeping to and fro
he lay there helpless, dazed with wounds.
'I cannot stand,' he said. 'My head works so.'

Hic iacet rex quondam rex que futurus.

This pitman tells his tale by rote, his dialect so shaly, cracked
it must be screened and panned and trimmed
like gravel, for nuggets of hard Fact.

On history's spoilheaps the shale of ideolect is tipped
by their Blue Book's terse compendium.
Voices crying: rex quondam rex que futurus sum.

On his true tongue, his dialect, his self
the door of documentary's locked fast shut.
Is sixteen. Is bound a putter. Cannot put.

THE APPRENTICE

Squeezed between elbows,
observing the rites and rituals
of a Masonic lodge, a masculine preserve,
the tools of their trade neatly arrayed.

The Worshipful Master, ex-matinee idol,
brilliantined hair and pencil moustache –
wizard with comb and scissors. Snip snip.
Follow feathers of hair drifting to the lino –
aftermath of a cat in consultation with a pigeon.

He cranks up the chair, nods in my direction –
short back and sides, not too much off the top.
It's over in minutes. Comb and scissors
find their place on the altar and a gentle fear
rises within me as the cut-throat razor
slides along a leather strop. Slip slap.

Head in a vice, fingers splayed on scalp –
Jimmy Cagney in the electric chair –
cold against my neck. Snick snack.
Finally the magic mirror behind my head.
Hot silvery coins wrested from my grasp
and I escape, fingers inside shirt collar
picking at shreds of fibreglass.

THIRTEEN SYLLABLES OF SAFETY

Georges Albert Eduardo Brutus Gilles de la Tourette
I wear the words around my neck like an amulet
That I can touch when I am tempted to disobey
The secret imperatives, as I have done today.
Their sound unifies certainty and coincidence
So that when duty is overruled by circumstance
And I do not perform my devotions properly,
Giving in to the inhibition of company,
Rejecting my script in favour of euphemism,
I say the names quietly, like a catechism
Which can save me no matter how far from grace I fall.
This is the last ritual; the one that pays for all.
This spoken, all manner of things shall be well with me.
But if unuttered, Venice will sink into the sea.

BADLY TRAINED

Dad was really keen on steam trains.
He drove them at weekends
Up and down a bit of track
With, like, a station at each end.

From noplace on to nowhere
And back again they go,
When was the garden to get dug?
My mum wanted to know.

I'm not so keen on steam trains.
In our house they made rows
Until dad gave up his driving
And its odd but I think of how

When we drive to Gran's with Sniffer
(He's our dog, I should have said)
He pushes out the window
And gets foam flecks on his head

And I remember picking dad up
From his little station, nearly dark
His face all soot and smiles
Like, if he'd been a dog, he'd bark.

CIVIL

Is this what you wanted to be, you ask
glass in hand, looking over my shoulder,
a civil servant? I may remember
years when the nib of your scorn held me fast
but you're not my lover now. Your lover
thinks otherwise, and that makes me smile, too.
Cheers, I reply. What would Quentin Crisp do,
disparaged in a restaurant, other
than remain polite and hoard the hard words?
Good job one of us is civil, sweetheart.

You take my hand in the gentrified square
and thank me, as I thank you, afterwards.
We're older than we were, too old to start.
I watch you walk away, glad you are there.

E.K.

I catch myself in the mirror,
a tired, hangdog stare -
my father's Hancock face,
his mad professor hair.

Cigar smoke signalled sojourns
in property law or tax,
constructing a deed or deal,
establishing the facts.

He'd lock onto a case, stay in
his dressing gown till three -
sometimes have his breakfast
after we'd sat down for tea.

He couldn't let go. Or lose.
Each word had to be *just right*.
He was Churchill in his finest hour,
Cromwell at his height:

his life was the law, his work.
He didn't do games, or chatter.
"Talk is cheap," he'd say. "It's the
written word that matters."

I see now we were more alike
than I used to like to think -
crafting words and drafting deeds,
joining up thoughts with ink.

But looking back, at him and me,
at so much that ended broken,
it's not the writing I think of now,
but the things we left unspoken.

BRINGING MUSSOLINI BACK TO ENGLAND

I flew into Rome to collect my liturgical vestments
and pick up a knocked-down Padre Pio in the New Year Sales
but I got side-tracked in *Via Del Clementino*
and chanced upon the head of Mussolini.
They wanted three thousand Euros for the *Duce*
but – hah!- I beat them down, I beat them down!

AL-MUSAYYIB

The houses are all the same,
low walls and shuttered windows.
Hard to imagine how the villagers survive –
scratching seeds into dust,
the desert singeing their heels.

Cars pass like seconds, never pausing.
The children are always busy,
boatbuilding from nothing
except rags and sticks and dreams,
sailing their yachts on oceans of sand.

The bomb was planted before dawn,
blankets of shrapnel glittering on the road.
A soldier from Alabama was killed outright,
nothing left to send back home.
The defence say his friends stopped thinking.

They kicked down the schoolhouse door.
The children were completing a test
heads down, remembering the alphabet,
pencilled letters marching right to left
in neat, unfinished lines.

CLOSE

I bent down,
touched the nearest fowl between the wings;
it crouched expectantly, shuffled
and I lifted it for Brenda.

I had been told she was my cousin,
pale, quiet, elfin,
from West Bromwich,
and this was the closest she had been to hens.

Her small hand caressed its neck,
felt the oily wax of wing feathers.
A cold claw fastened around my middle finger,
gripped it in bands of muscle,
tightened to a pulse.

A low crooning came from the raised throat,
the bright amber eye watched warily.
I teased the beak open,
exposed the thin tongue.

She fingered the wattles,
tracing their outline,
gently flicking them from side to side and smiling,
while I followed the line of the comb,
the pink, mapped skin rigid
between my thumb and forefinger.

She bent closer.
I caught the cleanness of her light brown hair,
her warm biscuit smell,
and as she took the fowl from me
she brushed my hand,
as light and soft as a day-old chick.

READING MY FATHER'S HAND

So much imagined, forgotten or never even known
comes down to me in these,
each one opening in the same formal way
I hope this letter finds you well, as its departure leaves me
learned no doubt on those rare days
when he chose school over poitín time in the bog
his hair black as the hops in the still, strong hands even then
that went on to haul bricks onto lorries in Oxford Street.
Trudging home through the smog to a silent room
where he laid down words on the plumb lines
of blue Basildon Bond like a row of McAlpine blocks.

Penned to them all the promise of what he earned, saved,
wired each week to the west of Ireland; decrying the days
when he couldn't work for the weather or the pain
and the ganger sent him back to his digs
that for thirty five shillings a week
gave him no light, no lock on the door
and the rain coming in through the roof.

I follow his shadow down the scaffold of each page,
where he names what it felt to be held
up against the wall with a knife blade of loneliness at his throat
and fight back with nothing but the brown neck of a bottle;
hear his voice in the cadence of Mayo accent
that even on paper carries a surfeit of syllable
in the word *childeren* that he had too many of.

Feel the loss in the hand that ended each one
with a crosshatching of kisses
no schoolmaster would ever have taught.

LAPWINGS

She found them
Lapwings
Strayed on the road
Three nestlings
Flattening into
Merging with stone
Yet not afraid
To be lifted and held –

Miracle –warm
New with life
Set down
With a stuck-on
Dagger beak.

Beside the verge
A fourth lay crushed
Broken
And blessed
And given.

And somewhere –
Not far –
A bird's unanswered
Peewit cries.

DO YOU WANT TO HOLD HIM?

"Do you want to hold him?" asked the nurse.
Why him, I wondered, this swaddled corpse,
Lifeless bundle of hospital waste.

"Do you want to hold him," she insisted,
"A last time?" There had never been a first.
What little life he'd had was incubated,
Fought and lost, a week of pain for him,
A lasting ache for us two looking on.
I had never held my baby live,
Was now too numbed to hold it dead.

The nurse, who'd perhaps sat vigil longest
Willing the damaged creature to survive
Gave me a look of incomprehension and contempt.
And held the folded blanket to my wife.
"Don't you want to hold him, say goodbye?"
As dazed as I, she took it nonetheless
And stared dry-eyed into the little face at rest.

I put a clumsy arm around her shoulders
Following her gaze, mute, awkward, frozen.
We should have been alone the three of us
She, me, it to wail and grieve or sit in silence.
The nurse exasperated snatched the baby back.
"Well, would you like to see the chaplain, then?"
She didn't understand our prayers had all run dry.

This was not the place for public grief or tears.
"Christ, no," I said, "not that!"
The first words I had spoken.

NOTES ON CONTRIBUTORS

Caroline Price studied music in York and London, now lives in Kent where she works as a violin teacher for Kent Music. Has always combined music and writing, and for 20 years has helped run the Kent and Sussex Poetry Society, based in Tunbridge Wells. Her poetry has been published widely in magazines and anthologies and has won many prizes. A third collection, *Wishbone*, is due to be published by Shoestring Press next year.

Jenny Morris writes poems and fiction. She has taught in this country and abroad. Her writing has won awards and appeared in many magazines and anthologies. Her latest poetry collection is *Lunatic Moon* (Gatehouse Press). She lives in Norwich.

Anna Davis: I graduated in art and design and am a tutor for the Open College of the Arts. I have been writing for about ten years. I have published a pamphlet *Wind Tied Door* based on the time I lived in the Outer Hebrides. Recently I had a couple of pages in 'North Words' magazine, and two poems were commended in the 2006 Brownsbank International Open Poetry Competition. I live near Edinburgh and continue to paint, teach and write, have three children and two cats.

Phil Powley began writing poetry after retirement as a lecturer in French. His work has been published in numerous anthologies and magazines and broadcast on BBC Radio 4. Themes that attract him are the two World Wars, nature and human folly. He builds tree houses for his grandchildren, scours the Solent marshes for seabirds and waders and plays golf only when desperate.

David Grubb has published poetry and fiction for many years. His latest poetry collection comes from salt this year; *It Comes With A Bit of Song*. Much of his recent work has been influenced by working in conflict zones and areas of extreme poverty such as Bosnia, Kosovo, Rwanda and Albania. He is currently seeking a publisher for a new novel and tutors in Creative Writing at Reading University, Norden Farm Arts Centre and the River and Rowing museum in Henley. He has also published short radio plays and edited anthologies of poetry and prose.

John Arnold was born in London in 1951. He now lives with his wife in East Sussex, has two grown up daughters and works as a town planner in local government. His poems have been widely published in literary magazines and anthologies, and have been broadcast on BBC Radio. He is a member of the Kent & Sussex Poetry Society.

Michael McCarthy grew up in West Cork, Ireland and has lived in Yorkshire for many years. He has recently returned from a Writing Residency at St Mark's National Theological Centre, Charles Sturt University, Canberra, Australia. His First Collection *Birds' Nests and Other Poems* won the Patrick Kavanagh Award in 1997 and was subsequently published by bradshawbooks, Tigh Fili, Cork. His Second Collection *Cold Hill Farm* is due out from Smith/Dorstop in autumn 2007.

Mike Casey is an Irish national, married with three sons. He was educated in New Ross, Dublin and Cambridge. He has worked in the Irish public sector and in Washington D.C. He has published a novel, *Come Home Robbie*, and a considerable amount of short fiction and poetry as well as articles for the Irish Times and Sunday Times.

Patrick Moran was born in Co. Tipperary, Ireland, where he still lives and works. His poems have appeared in most of the major Irish outlets e.g. Poetry Ireland Review, The Irish Times, Cyphers and The Honest Ulsterman. HIs work also featured in the inaugural *Forward* anthology (*UK: 1993*). He was also represented in the anthology, *Best of Irish Poetry 2007*. His first collection, *The Stubble Fields*, was published by Dedalus Press in 2001. A second collection is forthcoming in 2008.

Terence Brick was born in London in 1942. His poems have appeared in a variety of little magazines and anthologies including Envoi, Iota, Outposts and the S.E. Arts and PEN anthologies. He has broadcast on BBC Radio Medway, BBC Radio Berkshire and West Berkshire Radio. He is married with two daughters and lives in Newbury.

Gavin Stewart is an academic and new media artist. His last short collection of poetry, *Biology Lessons,* won the 1999 Poetry Monthly competition. His next collection *Ripening* will be published in late 2007. Gavin has designed a number of web-based texts including 'choice/cuts',

'Homecoming' and 'Slippage' (with the poet, Mark Goodwin). Gavin has recently completed a PhD on the aesthetics of computer-mediated textual art at the University of Bedfordshire.

John Foggin has been a teacher, lecturer, LEA advisor and author of books about teaching English. He gets excited about machine tools, and dreams of living on the Isle of Skye once they get a Rugby League team. Worked for a time with Andy Warhol in New York at the end of the 'Sixties. Represented in H.M.Government Art Collection. 'Shades of Grey' first poetry collection published by Boho Press in 2006.

Ann Drysdale was born near Manchester, raised in London, married in Birmingham, ran a smallholding and brought up three children on the North York Moors and now lives in South Wales. She was a journalist for many years, writing, among other things, the longest-running by-line column in the Yorkshire Evening Post. She has won a few prizes and published several books, including four volumes of poetry from Peterloo. The most recent of these, *Between Dryden and Duffy*, appeared in 2005.

Ian McEwen lives in Bedford with up to four children. He studied sciences, then philosophy and then worked in finance. Ian has just started to feel brave enough to let his poems out on their own, a few have appeared in *Smiths Knoll* and *The Interpreters House*.

Will Kemp studied at UEA and Cambridge, and has worked as a teacher, forester and environmental consultant in India, Europe, Canada and Australasia. He has had articles published in various journals, but wanted to develop his writing style more fully before seeking publication of his poems and short stories. He was shortlisted for the Keats-Shelley Prize in 2006, and has been published in Smiths Knoll (2007). He is currently studying creative writing with poet Carole Bromley at York University.

Julian Stannard is the author of *Rina's War* (2001) and *The Red Zone* (2007), both of which are published by Peterloo Poets. He has written a book about Fleur Adcock called *From Movement to Martians* and is soon to bring out a critical study of Donald Davie and Charles Tomlinson. He spent many years teaching at the University of Genoa and now lectures at the University of Winchester. He occasionally reviews for the Guardian.

Kate Rhodes was born in London in 1964. She has worked as an English teacher and has taught literature at English and American universities. Her first collection of poems *Reversal* was published by Enitharmon in 2005, and her second collection *The Alice Trap* will be published in 2008.

Jeremy Duffield: Derbyshire poet and playwright. His work has appeared in many poetry magazines and anthologies and he has had two collections published - *Danced by the Light of the Moon* and *Oak Apples and Heavenly Kisses.* He has recently begun dabbling in oils and watercolours, and can often be found sketching in cafes.

Geraldine Mills is a poet and short story writer, living in the west of Ireland. She has won numerous prizes for her work and has been published internationally in both genres. Bradshaw Books, Cork has published her two books of poetry, *Unearthing your Own* (2001) and *Toil the Dark Harvest* (2004) She has two books of short stories published by Arlen House. She is currently working on her third poetry collection to be published by Arlen House in 2008/9.

Madeline Munro's poems have appeared in *Ambit, Frogmore Papers, Links, The North, Scotland Alive Series, Stand, Understanding*: in S.E. Arts, Macmillan & UTP School anthologies, Virago New Poets: in *Sunday Telegraph Magazine*, National Poetry Competition Winners (Runners Up) and *The Independent* (Daily Poem). Broadcast on Radio Kent and Radio 3. Many of the poems in a collection *Lanterns in Hand* draw upon a farm upbringing in the Highlands when many animals on smaller farms were known by name and personality.

William Wood lives in Sussex. His poems and stories have appeared in several of the small magazines. This is the second year in a row he has had his entry in the Tonbridge competition commended. He would like to publish a collection of comic verse.

NOTES ON THE JUDGES

Ann Sansom's poems have appeared in the *TLS* and *The Guardian* as well as *The Virago Book of Wicked Verse* and the first ever Russian *Vogue*. Her latest book *In Praise of Men & Other People* (Bloodaxe), is "utterly compelling" (Poetry Review). Formerly Guest Poet at the *Times Educational Supplement*, Ann has taught at Leeds and Sheffield Hallam Universities and is a regular tutor with the Arvon Foundation and the Poetry Society's *Poetryclass*.

Peter Sansom's poems have appeared in *The Observer* and *PN Review* as well as on a billboard in Lancaster and *Women's Hour*. His latest book, *The Last Place on Earth* (Carcarnet) is 'quite brilliant' (*The Morning Star*). He is a director of The Poetry Business and editor of *The North* Magazine and Smith/Doorstop Books. Peter has been Fellow in Creative Writing at Leeds and company poet with both M&S and The Prudential. He was writer in residence at Tonbridge School in 2005

Worple Press is an independent publishing house that specialises in poetry, art and alternative titles.

Worple Press can be contacted at:
PO Box 328, Tonbridge, Kent TN9 1WR Tel 01732 368 958
email: theworpleco@aol.com.
website: www.worplepress.co.uk

Trade orders: Central Books, 99 Wallis Road, London E9 5LN
Tel 0845 5489911

TITLES INCLUDE:

Against Gravity – **Beverly Brie Brahic**
(A5 Price £8.00 ISBN 1-905208-03-0, pp. 72)

Full Stretch – **Anthony Wilson**
(Price £10 / 15 Euros ISBN 1-905208-04-9, pp. 104)

Sailing to Hokkaido – **Joseph Woods**
(A5 Price £6.00 ISBN 0-9530947-6-6, pp. 60)

Bearings – **Joseph Woods**
(A5 Price £8.00 / 10 Euros ISBN 1-905208-00-6, pp. 64)

'his work shows an impressive reach and range'   *Eiléan Ní Chuilleanáin*

'good and interesting poems well-presented'   *Books Ireland*

A Ruskin Alphabet – **Kevin Jackson**
(A6 Price £4.50 ISBN 0-9530947-2-3, pp. 88)

'you may like to consult *A Ruskin Alphabet* by Kevin Jackson, a collection of facts and opinions on ruskin and Ruskinites, together with a variety of pithy remarks from the man himself'   *TLS*

Looking In All Directions – **Peter Kane Dufault**
(A5 Price £10.00 ISBN 0-9530947-5-8, pp. 188)

'Wonderful stuff'   *Ted Hughes*

The Great Friend and Other Translated Poems – **Peter Robinson**
(A5 Price £8.00 ISBN 0-9530947-7-4, pp. 75)

Poetry Book Society Recommended Translation

The Verbals – **Kevin Jackson in Conversation with Iain Sinclair**
(A5 Price £12.00 / 20 Euros ISBN 0-9530947-9-0, pp. 148)

'Highly interesting.'   *The Guardian*

'Cultists will be eager to get their hands on it.'   *TLS*

'Worple Press have done it again… this sparkling introduction to Sinclair and his world.'   *The Use of English*

Stigmata – **Clive Wilmer**
(A5 Price £10.00 / 15 Euros ISBN 1-905208-01-4, pp. 28)

'a brilliant piece of work which brings honour to our time'

Sebastian Barker

Bowl – **Elizabeth Cook**
(A5 Price £10.00 / 15 Euros ISBN 1-905208-09-X, pp. 84)

'eloquent and profoundly humane'   *Martha Kapos*

A Suite for Summer – **John Freeman**
(A5 Price £10.00 / 15 Euros ISBN 978-1-905208-10-4, pp. 78)

'His poetry re-awakens a sense of wonder in us'   *Kim Taplin*

FORTHCOMING TITLES

To be In the Same World — **Peter Kane Dufault**

Warp and Weft — **an anthology of Worple writing**